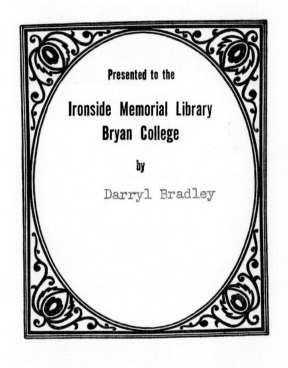

WE NEED YOU HERE,

PRAYERS FROM THE CITY

BAKER BOOK HOUSE • GRAND RAPIDS, MICHIGAN

WE NEED YOU HERE,

PRAYERS FROM THE CITY

ANDREW W. BLACKWOOD, JR.

TO MINETTE

CONTENTS

FOR THE CITY

heavenly Father
    you have started us on a journey
        from a garden to an eternal city
            where the streets are paved with gold and there is no night
                for your Son is the Light of it

today we live in a city
    surrounded by people you love
        some of them we love, some of them we don't
            here in this city the streets are not paved with gold
          in this city the darkness is intense
             because your Son is not the light

our city is caught up in a struggle for power
     the power of labor against the power of management
       the power of black against the power of white people
         the votes of the poor against the dollars of the rich
           too often we forget
               that the kingdom and the glory and the power belong to you
              not the best organized pressure group

you have placed us, the church, in this city
    and commanded us to overcome evil with good
        whether we are the church gathered or the church scattered
      in factories and banks and grocery stores
        and schoolrooms and offices and laboratories
          we have the unchanging duty to let our light shine
            so that others, seeing us, may glorify you

help us to do and say
   what will help our neighbors to see the light of Christ
   shining through us
      especially the neighbors we dislike and fear

when men of good will honestly disagree
   and men of ill will are trying
      to turn each disagreement into open hatred
      keep the Spirit of Christ in our hearts

Jesus loved the person on the other side of the fence
   help us to love the person on the other side of the fence
      Jesus cared for the hungry
      help us to care when your children are hungry
         Jesus respected the outcast
         help us to respect the outcast
         Jesus acted like your Son
            help us to act like your children

Christ is the Light of the world
   and we are called Christians
   help us to reflect his light
      we pray in his name
                  Amen

FOR CHRIST, IN THE MIDST OF PAIN

Christ

you have told us that you are present
   wherever God's children are in trouble or pain
      we find it easy to see you
         among the lepers and beggars in ancient Palestine
           help us to see you
              in the aches and pains of our own community

help us to see your face behind the empty grin
   of the panhandler who has lost his manhood
      help us to see you in the fright of the girl
         who has learned she is pregnant, and her boy-friend has run out
           on her
             help us to see you in the struggle of the colored man
               who is seeking a better life for his people
               and is doing all the wrong things

the siren shrieks at night
   what is it?
      heart-attack? fire? crime? accident?
      we don't know
         but we know somebody is in trouble
         and that's where you want to be

help us to hear you speaking
   through the screams on the picket line
      and the voice of the gabby old bore
         he's so lonely it hurts

help us to find you
in the girl who has turned her womanhood
from her glory into her shame
in the boy who is hooked on dope
in the pickpocket who is quietly being rushed off to jail

you were tormented by life
so is the mother whose twelve year old son
is hanging out with men she fears and distrusts
so is the policeman
accused of cowardice if he doesn't enforce the law
and brutality if he does
so is the salesman who has given up the struggle
between his conscience and his paycheck

forgive us, Lord
for keeping you forever back in ancient Palestine
quaintly puttering about and scattering sunshine wherever you went
if that were the truth
why would anyone bother to crucify you?

you plunged into the heartache of society
and you have told us
that's where we can find you today
we want a faith that will make us feel good
give us instead what you want
a faith that will make us care about others
we pray in your name
                                        Amen

FOR GRACE TO MEET PESKY LITTLE IRRITATIONS

Savior help us
   with the pesky little irritations
      that keep us from acting like Christians

if you would give us something big and glorious to do
   we like to believe we would do it
      with sparkle and dash
         and a rosy glow in the heart

but these pesky little things that bother us
   typewriter ribbons that don't work right
      and faucets that drip
         and shoestrings that break
            and cars that don't start

and these pesky people that bother us
   the idiot who toots his horn in the traffic jam
      and the neighbor who doesn't return the lawnmower
         and the newsboy who is late
            and the waitress who never gets anything straight
               and — dare we whisper it? — the members of our families

why do we have to act like Christians when we are irritated?
   why can't we be as stupid and inconsiderate as everyone else?

you were irritated, Jesus
   you got splinters in your fingers
      and people got on your nerves
         you could have kicked and screamed
            just like us
               but you didn't

you wanted to forget about God
    when you hit your hand with a hammer
        but you remembered
            then, when someone was driving a nail through your hand
                you still remembered
                    and prayed for the man who was killing you

maybe the minor irritations aren't so minor
    maybe through them you are preparing us
        for heavy duties and responsibilities
            help us, Savior

when things get out of order
    give us the gumption to fix them

when people get out of order
    give us the grace to remember that we are Christians
        and you really meant that bit about the turning the other cheek
            it's our job to try to be reasonable
                if we do our part, maybe the others will get the hint

remind us that we are Christians, Lord
    especially when we are irritated
        we pray in your name

                                                Amen

FOR COOL HEADS

Lord and Savior,

help us to keep our heads
   when so many people are loudly urging
     us to lose them
       when others cry wolf, help us to look
        and see if there really is a wolf
         before we start screaming too

where there is genuine danger
   help us to build defenses
     where there is none
       help us to tear down the walls of separation
       and to build instead foundations
        of honor and trust and understanding and charity

there is no need to remind you or ourselves
   of the dangers we face
     we do need to be reminded about the direction we are trying to go
       toward peace and cooperation within our country
        peace and cooperation among the nations of the world
         you told us that the way is rough
          forgive us for being so surprised
           when we find that you are right

everything is changing around us
   we easily get nervous and upset
     when we are rattled we do not always act with good judgment
       so help us to remember a few facts that remain always unchanging
       you have made this world
        you will win the final victory
         you have put us here to do our work
         and the heart of your work is charity
          mostly toward people we don't like
           keep these thoughts in our minds
           and we won't be so easily rattled

while others are screaming
   help us to think

we pray in your name
                      Amen

FOR GRACE TO STAND TALL

Jesus, friend of sinners
  help us to stand tall

you know the loads we carry
  you have carried them yourself
    loads of responsibility
      concern
        pain
         and guilt

where we have done wrong
  give us the honesty to admit it
    and the courage to confess it
    and the will to do right

where others have disappointed us
  help us to try to look at the world through their eyes
    if part of the reason for their failure lies in us
      then help us to straighten out what we can

when we are worried
  help us to sort out our thoughts
    is this thing worth worrying about?
      is this something that I can do something about?
      is my real worry a lack of faith in you?

when we are discouraged
  remind us that you rose from the dead once
    that your kingdom is coming and
      that you are still almighty
        you haven't given up this world
          and you haven't given up with any of us

we know that in the long run you will conquer every power of darkness
  conquer the darkness in us
    help us to walk in your light
      offering each action
        each word
          each thought to you

you went to a cross to help us over the rough places in the road
  guide us around the pitfalls
    and if we stumble
      help us to get up and stand tall
        and keep on walking with you

                                        Amen

FOR PRAYER

Savior, teach us to pray.

it is easy for us to bow our heads and rattle off words
    that mean nothing to us and
        probably don't mean anything to you either
            teach us, instead of aimless talking, to pray

help us to realize that prayer is our link with eternity
    when we pray we are coming face to face
        with the strongest force in this world
            we are entering into the heart of the mystery
            we are talking with God

so help us to approach prayer reverently and thoughtfully
    not giving our heavenly Father the snippets
        of time and attention we have left
            after taking care of everything we think important
            but bringing our best thoughts to him

help us to approach God honestly in prayer
    we see clearly what's wrong with everyone else
        but we are strangely blind to what's wrong in us
        we don't really want to give up
            the attitudes and habits that we find so comfortable

help us when we pray to focus our thoughts
    it doesn't mean much to pray for all mankind
        or all our enemies
            help us first to try praying for one person, one enemy
                then maybe we can do something specific
                about correcting one wrong in the world

you have told us that our faith will move mountains
    help us once in a while to give some of them a little push
        the mountains are so big
        and we are so small
            when we pray, our weakness
                is appealing to your strength
                so teach us, Lord, to pray
                              Amen

FOR THE MISSIONARIES

Lord Jesus
  you told us to go into all the world
    and proclaim the gospel to every creature
      we pray for our brothers and sisters
        who have left their homes
          and gone to the ends of the earth
            Point Barrow to Tierra del Fuego
              in obedience to your command

they grow lonely, Lord
  they miss the familiar sights and sounds
    they miss little things like baseball and hotdogs
      and they miss the big things
        their families and friends
          and good public schools
            and fine hospitals
              and free elections

they grow discouraged
  the human race has a remarkable resistance to the gospel
    it looks so much easier to go along
      not caring about you or the neighbor
        the statistical record of success is seldom impressive

they grow fearful
  the danger of being eaten by cannibals is remote for most of them
    and they must go to a zoo to see a tiger
      but there are other enemies
        who want to destroy the gospel and its earthly representatives

you were lonely and discouraged and fearful too
  but you followed the path of duty
    while they are following their path of duty
      walk at their side each day

they know that you care, Lord
  you have promised to be with them to the end of the world
    let them know that we care too
      we pray in your name
                                          Amen

FOR GUIDANCE

Father
> you get a great deal of excellent advice from your children
> > hear the prayer of those who don't know what is best
> > > we want to do the right thing
> > > > and everybody shouting at us sounds so confident
> > > > > but still we are confused and bewildered

we want to do the right thing between the nations
> what is it?
> > we hate violence and destruction
> > > we are sick at heart when men we love are caught up in the struggle
> > > > and we hate likewise the kind of government the enemy offers
> > > > > we can't agree with the hawks
> > > > > and we can't agree with the doves
> > > > > > show us what you want, Father
> > > > > > and help us to agree with that

and help us with the strife and turmoil in our cities
> everything we do seems to make everybody mad
> > so we are tempted to do nothing
> > > while little children starve and lonely old people die of neglect
> > > > we know we ought to be concerned about poor people's rats and plumbing
> > > > > but we don't know how we can best help
> > > > > we know that we ought to love our neighbors
> > > > > > but some of them are hard to love
> > > > > > > and some of them don't want our love

each one of us has private concerns
> that wake us up in the middle of the night
> > we have to make up our minds about something
> > and we don't know what to do

you led your children once through the trackless desert
> with a pillar of cloud and a pillar of flame
> > lead your children today
> > > help us to hear you call
> > > > this is the way, walk in it
> > > > > then, Father, help us to walk

we pray in the name of Jesus Christ our Lord
> > > > > > Amen

FOR WORSHIP

Father, help us to worship today
  not just to mumble a few hymns
  and say Amen in the proper places
    but to worship
      take us to the top of the mountain
        where Jesus' glory was revealed to his followers
      take us into the dark valley
        where he put his glory to work

open our eyes that we may see Jesus
  the battler for justice whom death could not defeat
  whose light will overcome every darkness in the world
  and whose love will conquer every hatred
    we keep trying to whittle him down to our size
    we want a tame, manageable Savior
    who will stay in the cradle forever
      help us to see Jesus as he looks to you
      and seeing him, to see ourselves

help us to examine our hopes
  is it enough to want a fat profit?
    give us hopes that are worthy of Christ's sacrifice
      teach us to hope that your kingdom will come to our city
      and that we may be able to speed its arrival

help us to examine our sins
  we can get terribly repentant about trifles
    show us our sins that matter
    and help us to repent of those

help us to look at this world you love
  why do you love us? how can you?
    we don't love one another
      help us this morning to try
      set us free from the littleness
        that fills so much of our lives
        enlarge our sympathy
          make us Christlike in our attitude toward others

we call ourselves Christians, followers of Christ
  help us to worship today
    by giving us a good square look at the Savior we are following
      in whose name we pray
                Amen

PRAISE

eternal Spirit
    we bow in reverence and awe
        before the miracle that you have worked
            in creating the starry heavens and the fertile earth

our minds cannot grasp
    the unbelievable distance of space
        where the planets and the suns and the galaxies
        whirl in their appointed courses

nor can we grasp
    the unbelievable delicacy of your work in nature
        where next year's leaves are folded in the autumn buds
            and next year's butterflies are waiting for the spring sun
        to bring them to life and beauty

far less can we grasp
    the mysteries that we cannot see
        where at your command
            the molecules and the atoms
                whirl in their courses

you have called us to live
    in this mysterious universe
        and surrounded us with other, darker mysteries

many of our brothers are in pain
    many of our brothers aren't even trying to do right
        many of our brothers are shut away from the rest of us by their
           color
            many of our brothers are shooting at each other
                many of our brothers live in grinding, debasing poverty
                many of our brothers live in fear

keep us always aware of the darkness
    keep us always aware of the light

for into this world, filled with beauty and terror,
    the Light of Light is shining
        Jesus Christ, the Son of God, has walked and talked with men

help us today to receive his light
    help us tomorrow to radiate his light
        into the squalor and horror of our time

we pray in the name of Jesus Christ our Lord

                    Amen

IN TIME OF CRISIS

eternal Father
    strong to save
        we need your guidance and wisdom
            to save our country today

save us from hysterics
    the tragedy is bad enough
        we don't need to make it worse by losing our heads
      save us from the stupid act
        help us to think

we are angry
    we want to strike back and take revenge
      save us from our feelings
      cool us down
        help us to seek and to find
        what will work
            not mere outlets for frustration

help us to look for justice
    remind us that we are a people dedicated to freedom
      and that our true freedom is to do your will

guide those who carry the heavy burden of responsibility
    while others are swearing at them
      teach us to pray for them

we live in a land where the people decide
    what is going to be
      Father, help us, the people of this land
        to pray for the right
          to search for the right
        to find the right
          to do the right

we pray for the sake of Jesus Christ

                        Amen

THANKS

eternal God

with our eyes wide open to the wrongs in the world
   we give you our thanks

thank you for bringing us into the world
   in this time of desperate need
      and giving us the responsibility
         to overcome evil with good
            and thank you for all the helps you have given
               toward fulfilling our task

thank you for our daily work
   and the strength and skill to do it
      thank you for the things you have entrusted to us
         — food and clothing and automobiles and dollar bills —
            we know, though sometimes we forget it
               that toil and its earthly rewards
                  are not the end of our striving
                     but a part of our reasonable service to you

thank you for all our spiritual blessings
   love and friendship
      loyalty and laughter
         truth and beauty

thank you for the land in which we live
   with its rich heritage of justice and freedom
      and the opportunity that lies always before us

yet, even as we thank you
  we recognize that these blessings can be lost
    others, more deserving than we, have lost them

so above all else we give our thanks
  for the blessing that man cannot take away
    yourself

we thank you, Father
  because you are always at work in the world
    where your children live
      and suffer

we thank you, Savior
  in the midst of our tribulations
    knowing that you have overcome the world

we thank you, Holy Spirit
  for the guidance you offer us
    and the victory of right that you have promised

teach us to live our thanks
  by working each day for the victory
    through Jesus Christ our Lord
                                        Amen

CONFESSION

eternal Father, strong to save, save us from our sins
we don't need to be saved from the sins
    that we aren't tempted to commit
        sometimes we let this blind us to our need for salvation
           from the sins of scribes and Pharisees and Christians

save us from getting so bottled up in ourselves
    that we forget our neighbors
        open our eyes and show us the pain all around us
        and what we can do to help

save us from our flimsy excuses
    if only we could live as well as we can explain our failure
      we would be Christians indeed
        we don't want to admit that we have ever been wrong
          so we pass the buck to everything and everybody
          we say no secrets are hid from your eyes
            give us some of your honesty in examining ourselves

save us from our weakness
    you know the difficulties we face
      help us to face them with you
        help us by showing us our neighbors
          who face far greater difficulties
           and still manage a smile or an encouraging word
            they have no strength that is not available to us
           Lord, make us strong

save us from feeling sorry for ourselves
    we know that we need your help
      when the deep waters threaten to engulf us
        but when we are paddling around in the shallows
          instead of boldly striking out like Christians
         we sulk because the water is too cold

save us from our laziness
    we are called the hands of Christ
      make us take his hands out of our pockets
        and do his work in the world
        we pray in his name

                            Amen

FOR STRENGTH

Christ, the Bread of life, feed us, for we are hungry
   Christ, the Water of life, quench our thirst
      Christ, our rest and our peace, calm the turmoil within us
      and make us strong

we ask for strength, not as a private luxury
   but because your work needs doing in the world
   and we are called here to do it

men and nations stand divided from each other
   we are called to tear down the barriers
      your brothers are hungry, in other lands and in this one
      we are called to feed them
         many of God's children have lost hope
         we are called to bring it to them
            by our words, our acts, and our example

keep fresh in our minds that you are the hope of the world
  not the Polaris submarine
   not the gold standard
     not this or that political leader
     but you, the strong Son of God

keep fresh in our minds that we are here to represent you
  if we are torn apart by tension and anxiety
    we can't be much help to anyone, including ourselves
     so fill us with the peace that passes understanding
     and lend your muscle to our weary bones

keep fresh in our minds that each decision we make
  is shaping the world, toward you or away from you
  and help us
    in the big decisions and the little ones
     to decide right
      we pray in your name

                             Amen

FOR THOSE WHO MOURN

Man of sorrows, acquainted with grief
  we pray for our brothers and sisters who mourn

we pray for each one who feels the keen grief that death can bring
  you have told us that death is not the end of life
    that beyond the grave is the resurrection
      yet you wept at the side of a grave
        you understand our grief
          strengthen those who mourn

we pray for our brothers and sisters who live in fear
  because someone they love is off at war
    and we pray for our brothers who are caught up in the cruel struggle
      praying that through their bravery the tortured people of the
        world
        may come to know the blessing of peace

we pray for our brothers and sisters
  who are shut off from the rest of society
    by their color or their accent
      if we are part of their trouble
        help us to correct what lies in our power to correct

we pray for each one who is in pain
  because of sickness or injury
    you knew pain so deep and intense
      that you thought the heavenly Father had forgotten you
        be the light for those who are in the valley of the shadow

we pray for those who are shut away from the rest of us
  because of a crime they have committed

we pray for those who are bored because of a stupid job
  we pray for those who are tearing their hair because the children get
    on their nerves
    we pray for those who bear the lonely responsibility of govern-
      ment
      we pray for those who are tortured by decisions they must
        make
        we pray for those who are tormented by the actions of
          someone else

compassionate Savior
  you have called us to represent you
    in compassion with your brothers and sisters who mourn
      you have done your part
        help us to do ours
          we pray in your name
                                        Amen

FOR THE CHILDREN

Lord Jesus

you came into the world a tiny little baby
  you kicked and squalled and carried on like any other baby
    you learned to crawl around the floor and how to stand up
    and how to walk, falling down most of the time
      just like the rest of us
        you learned first to babble and then to talk
          just the way we did
            you knew the joys and the pains of growing up
              just like every other boy or girl
                in this big, bewildering world

we pray now for every boy and girl in this world that you love

we pray for those who live in clean and happy homes
  where their fathers and mothers love them
    and provide healthy meals and a warm bed
      and send them to good schools

we pray for the boys and girls whose parents love them
  but cannot send them to good schools
    and cannot afford a decent roof overhead
      and cannot afford enough to eat

we pray for the boys and girls whose parents do not love them
  some are rich, some are poor, most are in between
    but they all need love
      help them, Lord Jesus, to grow up as healthy men and women
        don't let their minds become bitter and warped during these
          years

we pray for the boys and girls who live under decent government
  we pray for the boys and girls who live under horrible government
    in lands where cruelty and tyranny are taken for granted
      like the land where you were born
        lands where the policeman is an enemy
          lands where the rulers grow rich while the others starve
            lands where the people are fumbling about, looking for
              freedom
        and not knowing where to look

we pray for the boys and girls who are learning to love you
  we pray for those who are being taught the wrong things about you
  and especially for those who are being taught to hate you

we pray that the men and women of tomorrow
  may live in respect for one another
    with peace among the nations and within each nation
      the chances for peace on earth look dim
        but we remember that you grew up
          despite King Herod and all the others who wanted to destroy
            you
          grow in our world, and grow in us
        we pray in your name

                        Amen

LEAD US NOT INTO TEMPTATION

lead us not into temptation
   we say it over and over again
      sometimes the words skip right through our hearts
      and we forget that our thoughts and acts
      are part of your leading

lead us not into temptation
   we don't make the outward circumstance, that is your gift to us
   sometimes we like it, sometimes we don't
      but whether we like it or not
      the circumstance where we find ourselves
         is the place where you have called us to act like Christians

lead us not into temptation
   we have a great deal to do
      with the thoughts we think and the places we go
      and the people we talk to and the things we do
      when all these add up to temptation
         we sometimes act as if it is all your fault

lead us not into temptation
   we are grateful for the temptations that don't tempt us
      sometimes we say, there but for the grace of God, go I
      don't let us succumb to the temptation
      of looking down on the other person
         who has given in to desires that we don't desire
        that is one of the real temptations we face
        lead us out of it, Father

lead us not into temptation
   you have made us, male and female
      and filled us with deep longing to love and be loved
      and ever since this fact has complicated your world
         when people want the joys of love without the responsibilities
        teach us to dedicate our manhood or womanhood to you
        and to keep holy what you have made holy

lead us not into temptation
  we need things in order to live
    sometimes we live for things instead of for you
      when we get all mixed up about what is important
        lead us, Father, out of temptation
          help us to look at things, our things and the other person's
          as gifts from you
            designed to help us live like your children
            and not to keep us from it

lead us not into temptation
  you made people different
    male and female, black and white, Democrat and Republican, rich
    and poor
      we are tempted to despise the person who is different
        you don't want us all to look alike or think alike
          but you do want us to love one another
            when our differences tempt us toward hatred or scorn
              lead us, Father, out of temptation and into love

lead us not into temptation
  your way of leading is to send Jesus Christ into the world
    to live for us and to die for us
      so that we can live for you
        and when we are heading into temptation
          remind us of the Savior
            who climbed a steep hill to lead us out of it
            we pray in his name

                                          Amen

FOR HOPE

eternal God
>the help and the hope of our fathers
>help us today, and teach us to hope

everyone around us is singing the blues
>trouble in Asia
>>trouble in Africa
>>>trouble in Europe
>>>>trouble in Latin America
>>>>>trouble at home
>>>>>>trouble, trouble, trouble
>>>>>>>and they are right
>>>>>>>>the troubles are genuinely here
>>>>>>>>remind us, Father
>>>>>>>>>that you are here too
>>>>>>>>>>and you have appointed us
>>>>>>>>>>>to set right what we can

so much is wrong with the world
>and our efforts look so puny
>>that sometimes we decide to do nothing

don't ever let our faith blind us to what's wrong in the world
>let our faith guide us to the wrong we can right
>>evil will be conquered
>>>good will triumph
>>>>truth will overcome falsehood
>>>>evil is never the last word
>>>>the last word is love

teach us to hope for the day
>when the nations can work together
>>and the different races can respect each other
>>>and justice will rule between employer and employee
>>>>and people can enjoy themselves without destroying one an-
>>>>other
>>>>>and everyone will know that his neighbor is his brother
>>>>>because Jesus Christ is acknowledged as Lord

teach us that our efforts count toward Christ's victory
>even the cup of cold water counts
>>when it is given for his sake
>>>we pray in his name
>>>>>>>>>>>Amen

FOR DELIVERANCE FROM WORRY

God of mercy

you have offered us the cleansing and strength
    that come through prayer
        help us now, heavenly Father
           to pray
               and wash the doubts and fears from our minds

as we bow here in your presence
    each of us has burdens on the heart
        each of us is asking questions
           for which we seek a Christian answer
               where do I go from here?
                  what's going to happen?
               what must I do now?

all too often we forget our faith
    and give way to the luxury of worry
        mostly about things that never happen
           and things that are none of our concern
           and things we can do nothing about

forgive us, Father
    you have taught us to cast our burdens on you
        remind us to do so
           your shoulders are strong
             you can bear the loads
               that are too heavy for us

without the weight of worry that holds us down
    we can think, straight and clear
        we can see life steadily, and see it whole
        and where we best can represent Christ

help us daily to offer our best selves to you
    free from every kind of sin
        especially the sins that rise from doubt and worry
        we pray for Christ's sake

                                     Amen

FOR COURAGE

Father

we give our thanks for the men and women
  who go on doing their duty
    in the face of
      loneliness
        monotony
          misunderstanding
            danger

we pray for those who serve us in this city
  at hazard to their lives
    the policemen and firemen
      and all others whose work demands constant risk

we pray for the soldiers and sailors
  who at any moment are either bored or scared
    but they stay at their post and do what they must
      Father, bless their courage
        with the peace that they, and we, are praying for

forgive us, Father
  if we ever take for granted what others are doing
    so that we can live in peace and safety
      make us the kind of people who deserve these blessings

we expect others to show courage in the line of duty
  if, once in a while
    we must stand up to be counted
      and show a little courage of our own
        help us to set them an example
          by being the kind of people Christ has called us to be
            we pray in his name
                                    Amen

FOR VICTORY

Lord of hosts, mighty in battle
  forgive us for thinking that you lost interest in the human struggle
    about the time of the Hivites and the Jebusites — whoever they were
    and teach us, as we are fighting for the right today
      to look for your leadership and strength in the battle

we pray for our brothers, your sons, who are in battle today
  we pray for victory
    not so much the victory of arms
      as the victory of justice, the victory of law, the victory of peace

we pray for the tortured people who are being fought over
  that they may be able to harvest their crops in peace
  and send their children to school in peace
  and choose their rulers in peace

we pray for the troubled people of the world
  who today are living in fear of armies or armed gangs
  we pray for the victory over war, for everyone
  Lord of hosts, mighty in battle, give us peace

and we pray likewise for victory in the battles at home
  make the streets of our city safe from prowlers
  give us the victory over crime

help us to clean up the air we breathe and the water we drink
  give us the victory over dirt

you made the human race in different colors
  and today the different colored people stand and glare sullenly
  when they aren't actually shooting each other
    help us to do our part to speed the day
      when a man will be recognized for his worth as a man
      and not labeled in advance because of his skin pigment

in this beautiful city, with luxurious homes and soaring skyscrapers
teach us how to see and smell the slums
make us care about the rats and lice your children are living with
we know the difficulties of correcting bad conditions
forgive us when we make those difficulties into excuses
plan our campaigns for us, Lord
give us courage to fight against poverty
and lead us to victory

you told us once to subdue the earth and conquer it
and sure enough, we have invented lots of complicated machinery
that slowly is squeezing the humanity out of us
we are afraid to mutilate, fold, bend or staple a piece of paper
we park our courtesy when we get into an automobile
and kill fifty thousand or so of your children each year in
accidents
teach us to run machinery, don't let it run us
give us victory over the things we have made

all these are minor skirmishes, Lord, in the big battle
you made us free to choose between Christ and self
and you knew that the choice will always be hard
help us to win that biggest victory, the victory of Christ
over our own selfishness and pride and greed
then our lives
instead of stalling it off
can hurry along the final victory of Christ
over everything that is wrong in the world
we pray in his name

Amen

FOR THE HOLY SPIRIT

eternal Spirit
    Lord and Giver of life
        we turn to your eternal calm
            from the storms of life
                not asking that we may forget the storms
                    but seeking strength to man the ship

quiet the noise of our daily lives
    still the tumult of our restless spirits
        smooth the rough places in our troubled hearts
        and let us hear the Savior's voice
            peace, it is I, be still

speak to our memories
    keep reminding us of family and friends
        who have helped us along the way
            and remind us often of those times in the past
                when we knew that you were very close

speak to our faith
    we know that Jesus Christ has come into the world
        to be victor over everything that is wrong with the world today
            we say it over and over again on Sunday in church
                sometimes we forget it when we leave the house of worship

speak to our consciences
    may some clear word of direction come to those
    who are traveling a wrong road, and know it
    and speak a clear word to those
    who are traveling a wrong road, and don't know it
    show us our shabby excuses
    our vile tempers
    our bitter words
    and our treasured hatreds
    show us where we are wrong
    and help us to lay our sins on the cross

speak to our hopes
    helping us to look beyond the things we need
    and to hope for what Jesus hoped for us
    charity toward our neighbor
    a sense of direction through life
    and the knowledge that you are always near

speak to our decisions
    speak to the big ones, where we wrestle in agony
    trying to make up our minds
    speak to the little ones that we think unimportant
    yet each decision we make today, big or little
    helps mold our characters tomorrow
    help us, each time we choose, to choose life

we pray in the name of Jesus Christ our Lord

                Amen

FOR THE PRESIDENT

King of Kings, and Lord of Lords

we pray for a Father's blessing
    on the President of the United States
        you will reign forever and ever
            he can rule just a few short years
                but those years are important to us
                and to the rest of the world
                and we believe to you

our President did not create the mess we are in
    he inherited it, and is dealing with it as wisely as he can
        of course we could do much better
            but since our nation has seen fit to call him
                and has neglected to call us to this high office
                give us the grace to pray for him
                he has enough critics already

we cannot agree with everything he does
    and when we get to heaven we can find out who was right
        today we ask you to give him wisdom
            to choose the right advisers
                and to deal with the right issues
                and to ask the right questions
                and to find the right answers

help him in his search for peace among the nations
help him in his search for peace within this nation

give our President courage, Lord
    it is easy for him to grow discouraged
        and give him strength to bear his many burdens
            make us burden-bearers with him
                and not that much more trouble for him to carry around

above all else, give him faith
    keep clear in his mind that you are in charge
        and that none of his plans can succeed unless they are your plans
        your kingdom is eternal
            help him to build for eternity

let him give the best he has to each day
    then give him a sound sleep at night
        with the knowledge that people like us are praying for him
            so that he can wake up refreshed
                to give his best to tomorrow
                    we pray in the name of the Prince of peace

                          Amen

FOR THE RIGHT THOUGHTS

Holy Spirit, fire of God
  burn within our minds

teach us to draw the line between forethought and worry
  we know that we ought to think and plan
    we know that we ought not to worry and fret
      but usually we worry
        and it's mostly about things that we can't control
        and things that never happen

teach us to cast our burdens upon you
  and to trust, even in the valley of the shadow
    then, with our minds free and clear from the disease of worry
    we can give our best thought
      to whatever we may face

give us sense enough to slow down and think
  long enough to see the difference
    between what is important and what is trifling
      and then to concentrate our time where it matters

help us to think about our neighbors
  they have reasons for their many faults
    forgive us, maybe we are part of the reason
      why they act the way they do
        give us grace to forget
          the harsh word spoken to us
            and to apologize for
              the harsh word we have spoken

help us to think about those we love
  and remind us, once in a while
    to tell them so
      we pray in the name of the Lord of love

                                        Amen

TO THE HOLY SPIRIT

Spirit of the living God
    burn in our hearts today

we do not ask for a vision of heaven
    with the sky all lit up
        just keep a steady glow in our hearts
            so that we will care about the things that matter

you have told us that you are always near
    closer than breathing
        nearer than hands and feet
            teach us how to recognize you

when we struggle with conscience, you are close
    closer, sometimes, than we really want you

when doubts rise in our minds, you are close
    helping us to think
        not doling out the soothing syrup we want

when the way is rough and uphill, you are close
    often we forget where we are going
        you know the way
            make us strong to get there

teach us to see the divine flame
    wherever there is joy or peace or true freedom
        teach us likewise to see the divine flame
            in the midst of our pains and sorrows
                we are supposed to look at everything through the cross
                    remind us, when we need it

you are always at work in our hearts
    help us always to work with you
        through Christ our Lord

                                        Amen

FOR THE CHURCH

Father, we come to your church to find you
 as if you needed to be found
  the whole earth is full of your glory
   the starry heavens and the blossoming earth proclaim it
    no place is so lonely or barren or neglected that you are shut
     out
     and yet we come to your church to find you

we come to a place that is dedicated
 where every detail of the building and the service
  sing aloud to our deaf ears that you are God

we gather with our friends and neighbors
 to share their faith
  when ours is weak, to receive
   when ours is strong, to give

we meet in a building
 where your children learn about you
  where men and women unite their lives in holy marriage
   where infants receive the blessed sign of citizenship in your king-
    dom
    and where we offer our thanks for the lives of those
     who have left the earthly church for the eternal church
      a building filled with memories, some happy, some sad
      but all pointing to you

when we are in the building
    tell us that you are everywhere
        while we are met with a few of your children
            tell us again that your church is wrapped around this whole world
            if we belong to your church here
                we belong to your church everywhere
                    if your church anywhere suffers, teach us to share the pain
                        if your church anywhere rejoices, teach us to rejoice

while we are in your church, give us a glimpse of your glory
    that will help us to see your glory every day
        in the unfolding flowers
            in our daily toil
                in all laughter and loyalty and love

and where your glory is obscured
    by the tensions and pains and sorrows of our community
        show us how to radiate your glory
            where it is most needed
                we pray for Christ's sake

                                        Amen

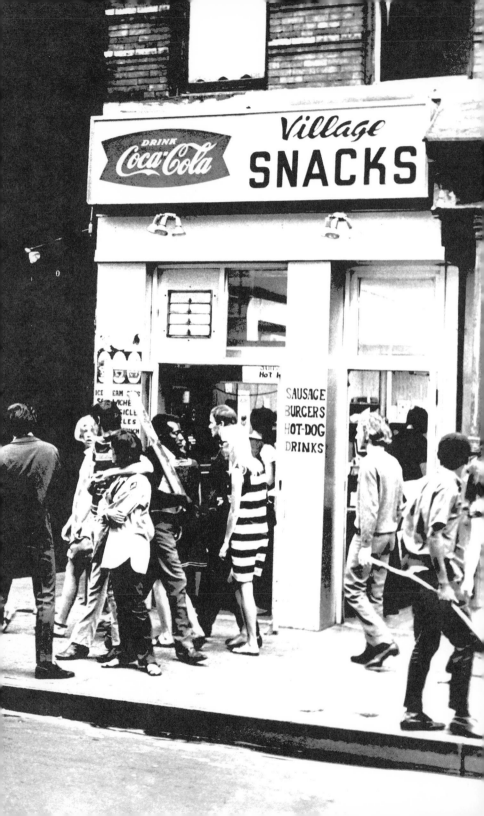

FOR OUR BROTHERS WHO HAVE SINNED

Jesus, Friend of sinners
   we pray for our brothers and sisters who have sinned

we pray for those who have sinned and know it
   for each who has done wrong in a moment of blind passion
     for each who has given in to a weakness
      for each whose judgment has been warped
        by greed or jealousy or hatred
          for each who struggles with a degrading habit
          and for each who has given up the struggle

likewise we pray for those who have sinned and don't know it
   for each who is blind and deaf to the need about him
     for each who is indifferent to his neighbor's pain
      for each who has failed to do the right
        for each who is smugly satisfied
          for each who is so busy with things
            that he has no time for you

as we pray so thoughtfully for those who have sinned
   remind us that we too are sinners
     we too have been arrogant
     we too have been weak
      we too have been blind and deaf

open our eyes
   let us see where we have done wrong
     or failed to do right
       give us courage to admit our wrong to you
       and where necessary, to our neighbor

forgive the wrong we have done
   then we may be able to help our neighbors
     straighten our their lives

and put us back on the path that leads to eternal life
   we pray in your name

                         Amen

FOR LOVE

God of love
  you made this world
    where the miracle of love takes place
      where children are surrounded by love from their birth
        and families are guided by love each day
          and aged people are upheld by earthly love
            until they enter at last into your eternal love

we are grateful
  that so often your plan for earthly life
    is carried out
      the kingdom of heaven is not way off somewhere else
        but wherever people live in response to your love
          thank you, Father
            for every outpost of the kingdom
              here in our city

while we give thanks for what is good
  we would not forget what is wrong

we pray for your sons who are marching to war
  God of peace, guide us into paths of peace on earth
    we pray for the families that have suffered cruel loss
      God of comfort, comfort them
        we pray for those who will bear the scars of war through life
          let us never accept their sacrifice unthinking
          help us to strive for a world
            where young men, each loving his own land
              will work together and not fight one another

open the locked doors in our hearts
　　and let us share your love for your children in desperate need
　　　　for those who want to work and don't know how to hold down a job
　　　　　　if our background was as poor as theirs, we wouldn't do very well
　　　　　　　　either
　　　　　　　　for those who want a good education for their children
　　　　　　　　　and aren't getting it
　　　　　　　　　　if we grow irritated with the way they act
　　　　　　　　　　　remind us of the irritations they have endured
　　　　　　　　　　　　it's hard for us well-fed Christians to believe
　　　　　　　　　　　　　but not very far from us little children are faint-
　　　　　　　　　　　　　ing
　　　　　　　　　　　　　because they don't have enough to eat

in our beautiful city
　　husbands and wives are snapping and snarling at each other
　　parents are careless about their children
　　　　who grow up without respect for their parents or anyone else
　　　　young people are making cheap the holy mystery of love
　　　　　　employers and employees are trying to gouge one another
　　　　　　old people are lonely and neglected

disturb our calm, Father
　　with the cry of pain in our community
　　　　and make us channels through whom your love
　　　　　　can reach the lives of those who are desperate to know you
　　　　　　　help us to live so that they will want to love Jesus Christ
　　　　　　　in whose name we pray

　　　　　　　　　　　　　　　　　Amen

FOR TODAY

Jesus, the Road and the Truth and the Life
  help us when we lose the way
    help us when our minds are wavering and doubtful
      help us when we are bruised and weak and ready to give up

Jesus, the Road, your way is rocky and uphill
  you climbed the rocky path and found that it leads beyond the stars
  help us to climb
    especially when the top of the hill is hidden from us
      by mists and fogs

Jesus, the Truth, you know the doubts that crowd our minds
  we can see and touch and taste the world around us
    but God is invisible, and sometimes we wonder where he is, if any-
    where
      our way of doing things looks sensible
        and, others have told you before, yours looks impractical

Jesus, the Life, if the way you lived is the way we ought to live
  we aren't very healthy
    we get excited by things that bored you
      and bored by the things you thought important
        we laugh at the wrong jokes
          and admire the wrong things, chiefly in ourselves

yet in spite of the way we stumble along
    you don't always keep striding ahead
        you are with us when we get lost
            and when our thoughts are farthest from you
                you are here to heal us, if we are willing to be healed

you are our Friend
    ready to give us a boost when we stumble
        ready to clear up our tangled thoughts
            ready to cool our fevers and thaw our chills

so, with all our faults, which you know far better than we know them
    we come asking
        help us to walk straight and steady today
            help us to get our facts straight today
                help us to stand tall and to breathe deep and to be
                    real Christians in each word and each act and each desire
                        today

we are glad that we can pray to you
    you share all our weakness
        help us to share your strength

we pray in your name

                                        Amen

FOR STEADFASTNESS

while we walk in darkness, Father
  we know that a steady light always shines
    in the unclouded heaven
      we are caught up in the storms
        with you is eternal peace

breathe your life and peace into us
  so that we may be free from fear
    so that we can keep our heads in the midst of conflict
      so that we may be steadfast when others waver
      and so that we can be peacemakers
        in this turbulent world that you love

grant that we may never be puffed up with our own importance
  and grant that we may never despair when things don't work out our
    way
    in time of success and in time of failure
      you are God, always the same
        you have bound us to yourself and we are yours
          when we want to stretch the bonds, draw them close
          and keep us safe from pride or from despair

when things go the way we like, we loudly sing your praise
  you are faithful and kind, your power upholds us and encourages us
    when our plans turn upside down, you still are faithful and kind
      sometimes rods and stripes are the bitter medicine we need
        a wise father does not indulge his childrens' foolish desires
          when you are stern, it is because you love us
          and are making us ready for eternal life

think for us better than we can think for ourselves
  help us to think your thoughts with you
    and when we disagree, give us a little sparkle of grace
      that will teach us to compare our ignorance with your wisdom
      and will give us a little chuckle at our foolishness
      and will get us back on the road that leads to life

we pray in the name of Jesus Christ our Lord

                Amen

FOR JOY

God
    who created smiles and laughter
      fill our faith with joy

we take our religion most solemnly
    and put on our unhappy expressions when we come to church

forgive us, Lord
    we think about our faith as
      pleasant things that must not be done
        and unpleasant things that must be done
          give us back the joy that we seem determined to lose

open our eyes and let us see the light
    we are Christians, we have something to be joyful about
      you are almighty
        not the powers of darkness ranged against you
          your kingdom is coming
            and we can be part of the final victory

chase away the gloom from our hearts
    blow away the cobwebs of
      doubt
        gloom
          worry
            and depression

the Light of the world is shining
    let him shine in our hearts
      and let him shine through our lives
        into the sordid and dismal places of the world
        work a miracle in us
          and change us gloomy Christians
            into bearers of Christ's radiance

          we pray in his name

                    Amen

FOR HONESTY ABOUT OURSELVES

Lord Jesus
  our Savior, our Friend, and our Judge

help us to judge ourselves
  as skillfully as we usually judge everybody else
    we see what others are doing wrong
      or failing to do right
        and are brimful of ideas for their improvement
          but examining ourselves is painful

Light of the world
  shine in our hearts
    and let us see all the dust under the dresser
      and the junk lying disordered in the corner of our lives
        help us to see our prim Christian sins
          as clearly as you see them

we aren't hijackers and we don't peddle dope
  but

we are swift to criticize and slow to help
  we love to feel important
    and we use other people to make us feel that way
      we get all confused about what is gold and what is tinsel
        we waste a lot of time on second-rate things
          we grumble so much about what is wrong
            that we are ungrateful for what is right
              we take other people, and even you, for granted
                we are greedy, forgetting that this is your world, not
                  ours
                    we are ready to believe anything about anybody
                      providing it's bad enough
                        we don't spend anywhere near the time
                          seeking your company
                            that we spend avoiding it

shine in our hearts and let us see ourselves
    then we can admit to ourselves, and to you, that we need help
    then we can give you each shabby thought and desire
    and everything else that clutters our lives

then, instead of advising others how to live
    we can show them what it means to be Christian
    Light of the world
        shine in us and through us
           today
                              Amen

FOR CHARITY

almighty God

Giver of every good gift
  we pray for that supreme gift
    without which the others are worthless
      the grace of charity

help us to be patient when the going is rough

when we are tempted to envy those who have more
  remind us of those who have less
  and help us to be charitable toward both

give us a fit sense of proportion
  about our own importance
    and our neighbor's

teach us to be courteous when others are friendly
  and courteous when others are difficult

guard us against the greed that easily corrupts our minds
  keep our tempers under your control
    guide our eyes, our ears and our hearts
      toward what is true and good and clean
        rather than the evil that, at first
          looks more exciting

make us strong to carry the load a Christian should carry
  make us wise to distinguish between truth and half-truth
  and to hold fast the truth
    give us the hope that comes from faith
      and keep us in that faith
        so that our neighbors, and you
          can depend on us

we pray for the grace of charity
  not an airy abstraction up in heaven somewhere
    but the practical grace of Christlike living today
      we pray in Jesus' name

                    Amen

FOR A SHARP FOCUS ON LIFE

heavenly Father, we call you our Creator
  you made our hands and feet and eyes and ears
    for which we give our thanks
      and you made, deep down in each one of us
        a need for you
          sometimes we remember to thank you because we need you
          sometimes we forget

sometimes we meet the need the only way it can be met
  by turning to you in faith
    and dedicating our hearts
      our souls
        our minds
          our strength
            to you

and sometimes we set up god-substitutes
  we worship the tools you gave us to work with
    we put ourselves and our wants at the center of the picture
    we forget about you and our neighbors
    and then we wonder, plaintively,
      why there is that God-shaped emptiness in our lives

long ago a troubled child of yours cried
  I believe, help my unbelief
    and we join our voice to his
      we hope, help us when we despair
        we have received the peace that passes understanding
          help us when we battle with ourselves and our neighbors
          we love, help us when we fail to love
            we need you, help us when we think we can live with-
            out you

we pray in the name of Jesus Christ our Lord

                      Amen

FOR A SOLDIER, KILLED IN ACTION

Man of sorrows, acquainted with grief
  we pray for your brothers and sisters who mourn

you have told us that beyond the dark clouds is the eternal light
  and beyond the grave is the resurrection
    yet you wept at the side of a grave
      you understand and share our grief
        strengthen those who mourn
          and help them to hear you say
            I am the Resurrection and the Life

we pray for your brothers and sisters who live in fear
  because someone they love is off at war

we pray for your brothers who are caught up in the cruel struggle
  praying that through their bravery and sacrifice
    the tortured people of all the world
      may know, at last, the blessing of peace

we pray for your brothers who know the heavy responsibility of leader-
ship
  the generals and the admirals, and our civilian leaders with the
    State Department
    especially we pray for our President
      asking you to guide and encourage him
        as he seeks an honorable end to the bitter struggle

never let us accept the sacrifice
    of those who have given their lives so that we might live
      without dedicating ourselves once more
        to the cause for which we battle
          the reign of law among the nations
            the right of the small nations to work out their destiny in
              peace
              others have given everything for this cause
              help us to give what we can

kindle again in us the fire of faith
    that death is not the end but the doorway into eternity
    and that this dying world
      will become the living kingdom of Christ

in this faith we commit to your eternal keeping
    the life of one whom we have known and loved for a while on earth
    through Christ our Lord

                        Amen

FOR THE GOVERNOR

King of kings and Lord of lords
  we ask your blessing
    on the Governor of this state

where he is right, strengthen him
  where he is wrong, correct him
    give him the wisdom, the courage, and the strength he needs
      to do your will in these troubled times

help us who are citizens of this state
  to remember that government is everyone's business
    not just that of the politicians
      they have their responsibility
      we have ours

it is easy for us to sit back and sneer
  at the mistakes others are making
    it is no trouble to be a good quarterback
      while sitting in the grandstand

we want more and more service from the government
  teach us to enjoy paying more and more taxes
    we want strict law enforcement for everyone else
      why does our zeal flag when we get behind a steering wheel?

we want the poor people to behave
  and the school teachers to be satisfied with their wages
    and the hippies to get a haircut
      and the doves to grow talons
        and the hawks to coo gently
          and we blame the Governor when we don't get what we want

help us to hear the cry of pain in our state
and where we can to ease the pain
then we might make the Governor's burden a little lighter

help us to set him a good example of the right attitudes
that is more difficult, but somehow more important
than telling everyone how wrong he is

we are Christians, redeemed by Christ
called to be Christ's agents of redemption
unfortunately, we are better at tearing people apart
than we are at putting things right
overcome our weakness
give us Christ's strength

help us to support our Governor when we can
and when we must disagree
help us to do it in charity
remembering that we are Christians
even when we talk politics
we pray in the name of Jesus Christ, our Lord

Amen

FOR THE GENERAL ASSEMBLY

gracious God
    you have helped your church in ages past
      our only hope for the stormy present is with you
        you are the refuge to whom we turn when exhausted
        and our strength when we turn back to our work
          you are our vision and courage when we are fearful
        at all times and in all seasons
        you are our Father

in the faith of the earthly fathers that lives still in us
    and the power of hope that Christ brings
      we ask your blessing on the General Assembly of our church

grant to the commissioners
    a clear knowledge of what is wrong in the world
    a renewed vision of your glory
      a fresh confidence that Christ can rebuild what man has destroyed
        a deep awareness that you are working out your eternal pur-
          pose
          a firm conviction that the church is in the world to serve
          and Christ's own burning desire that the church may
            be one

grant to all the church
    the joy and peace of believing
      so that in our day of gloom and strife
        we may bring this joy and peace to others
          proclaim through us
            the good news that can bring life to the dying world
            we pray in the name of Christ
            the only Head of the church
                        Amen

FOR HEALTH

Holy Spirit
   Lord and Giver of life

we ask the blessing of health
   for our brothers who suffer
      in body, or mind, or spirit

we pray for those who minister to human ills
   the physicians and nurses
      those who carry out the monotonous duties of administration
         those who toil in lonely laboratories
            to learn the cause and the cure of disease

we pray for those who watch and wait
   beside their loved ones who suffer

help us all to remember
   that God is in the valley of the shadow
      and that, although we have tribulation in the world
         Christ has overcome the world

we do not know why pain and grief come into our lives
   but when they come, Holy Spirit
      enable us to be brave
         lifting our thoughts to you
            for courage, strength, and help
               through Christ our Lord
                                                Amen

THANKS FOR THE INCARNATION

Lord Jesus
    you came to earth a long time ago
      almost nobody was really expecting you
        almost nobody recognized you when you came
          and when the eternal light shone from your face
            men closed their eyes and refused to look

shine in the darkness of our troubled souls
    and help us to be as bright as the shepherds were
      when they went to look where you were
      and not where people expected God to be

we pray for the troubled, tortured world
    so desperate for your love, and so ready to reject it
      we pray for the victims of war, the exiled, the hungry
      we pray for your brothers who live under tyranny
        you came to be the Prince of peace
        win your victory in our hearts
          and help us to win your victories in the world

we pray for each family
    for those who are separated because of war
      for those where there is sickness or loss
        for those where there is strife or shame
          for those who must make hard decisions
            Lord Jesus, you lived in a family on earth, you know all our
              needs
              you want to be the older brother, living in each home
              help us to want you living with us

we pray especially for those who think they are beyond the reach of
    your love
    who have done something they are ashamed to admit, even to you
    and they think you have no use for them
        tell them, Jesus, that's why you came to earth
        because there's darkness in every soul
        and you haven't given up with any of us

your birth was a miracle and your life was a miracle
    work that miracle in us
        teach us to care for the other person the way you care for him
        teach us to trust our Father the way you trust him
        give us some of your courage
        give us some of your strength
        and when the night gets dark
        give us a song to sing

we pray in your name

                                        Amen

PRAISE

eternal God
    Creator of the starry heavens and the earth
        you are far beyond the reach of our highest thought
      a mystery we dare not approach
        yet you have asked us to call you Father

you do not need our praise
    but we need to praise you
      so that we can find ourselves
        by being lost in you

while we are at worship
    show us how great you are, and how great is our need for your help
      our lips say easily that you are almighty
      our hearts, sometimes, are slow to believe it
        you spin the stars in their courses
        you can guide us through life
          if we are willing to be guided

the heaven of heavens cannot contain you
    and yet you want to live in the heart of each one of us
      don't let our praise be just words
        help us to want you living in our hearts
      we pray in Jesus' name

                        Amen

FOR OUR CITY

Savior
   long ago you wept over Jerusalem
      but you dried your tears
         and plunged into the midst of the city
            where you lost your life
               helping your friends to live

we need you in our city today
   we need you in the factories
      we need you in the offices
         we need you in the slums
            we need you in the suburbs
               we need you in the courts, and the schools, and the grocery
                  stores
               we need you

our city is gripped by fear
   when people are afraid they strike out blindly
      everyone is afraid that someone else will strike out
         can you speak to us as you spoke to your friends in another storm?
         peace, it is I

can you give us cool heads to think with?
   and warm hearts to love with?
      can you live in our midst?
         we have seen what happens when we push you away
         live here, make our city your city
            a place where people will respect each other
            and live together in peace

we pray for your servant the mayor
   we pray for your servant the chief of police
      we pray for your servant the governor
         we pray for your servant the president
            give them wisdom, compassion, and strength
            and give them levelheaded people to govern

help us, the church in this city
   to be the church, the body of Christ
      the people who so love you that we live our love
         the people who care about their neighbors
            the people who are overcoming evil with good
         we pray in your name
                         Amen

TEACH US TO PRAY

Lord
    teach us to pray

teach us to pray in church
    where the music and the architecture and everything else
      help focus attention on you

teach us to pray in our homes
    where every stick of furniture and every pot and pan
      can stir up memories
        sometimes happily
        sometimes not

teach us to pray at our daily work
    dedicating each task to you

teach us to pray while we are enjoying ourselves
    — or trying to —
      and give us the gumption to stay away
        from any enjoyment we cannot share with you

teach us to pray when we are happy
teach us to pray when we are blue

Lord
    teach us to pray

in our better moments we know that prayer is more than words
    sometimes we get so wrapped up in words that we aren't praying at all
      sometimes we rattle off words without letting them bother our hearts
      make our word our bond when we pray

don't ever let us stop with asking for daily bread and that sort of thing
    you know our wants, you created them
      and we don't need to apologize for them
        but teach us to reach beyond our normal, self-centered desires
        and to want above everything else
          to live for you

teach us to pray with our lips
    so that our lives may be a prayer
      we pray in our Savior's name

                Amen

FOR FAITH AS WE CONFRONT DEATH

heavenly Father
   we are grateful for a faith
      that teaches us to look toward the eternal light
         beyond the lowering storm cloud

we are grateful that beyond the dark cloud men call death
   is a light that man did not kindle
      and man cannot put out

we are grateful that our Savior Christ
   has lived on earth with us
      and mapped the way to eternal life

we bring our sorrow to you
   but undergirding our sorrow is our hope
      we know that part of us is dust and will return to dust
         and part of us is spirit
            you have taught us to hope, where we cannot prove
               that the spirit will return to God who gave it

we are grateful for the ties of earthly love that now are broken
   we are grateful for our faith in the unbreakable ties of eternal love
      help us to live in this faith and hope
         so that we may live in heaven with those who have gone before us
            and with our Savior
               in whose name we pray

                                             Amen

THANKS

thank you, Father, for being God

our hearts are burdened
  by the strife among the nations
    and the strife within our land
      and each of us has private sorrows
        known only to ourselves and to you
          still, burdens and all, we give our thanks

we are grateful because you are God

thank you for letting us know something about you
  through the glory of a crimson sunset
    and the wind blowing through the pine trees
    and the clear song of the cardinal
    and the laughter in the eyes of a child

thank you for telling us more about you
  through the message of your love and our duty
    in the holy Bible
      but mostly we give our thanks for the gift of your Son
        who came to this world to lead us into the eternal world

thank you for your forgiveness
  with you we have a second chance
    thank you for your gifts of health and strength
    thank you for the material blessings
      that make spiritual life possible on earth
      we appreciate these blessings
        but chiefly we are grateful
          that you are at the heart of this universe
            not the blind interplay of soulless force
            but you, our Father

help us today
  when the world is dying on its feet
    because it does not know your love
      to live our thanks by telling others
      that you are our Father
        and Christ is our Brother
          and life in this mixed-up world has a goal
            that we can reach and help others to reach
          through Jesus Christ our Lord
                Amen

FOR OUR WORK

Jesus, Carpenter of Nazareth

thank you for the gift of work
  our blessing, not our curse

whenever we drive a nail straight
  or add the figures correctly
  or wash the dishes clean
    that is part of our worship

stand at our side each day
  and lighten its small duties with your presence
    and by your light show us what is really important
    we live and work in the world
      may we never live and work for the world
      our daily toil is not the end of life
        but one of the ways we build for eternity

help us to give our best to the task at hand
  if it is monotonous and boring
    remind us of the people whose needs we are meeting
    and the Father whom we are serving
    and keep us cheerful

guard us against shabby workmanship
  guard us against leaving things half done
    guard us against skimping where it doesn't show

help us rather to labor
  so that when our earthly tasks are done
    we may hear you saying
      well done, good and faithful servant
        enter into the joy of your Lord

Amen

IN TIME OF STRIFE

Lord and Savior

save us from the bitterness and horror of violence
   and bring from the tensions of today
      understanding between those who are opposed
         so that your brothers of every race and class
            may work together for justice
            and may find workable answers
               to the questions that torment us

help us, when we read the newspaper
   to remember that you are not nearly so helpless
      as we usually think you are
         you know all about trouble on earth
         you have been this way before
            you know the way through the dark valley
            into the upland light

keep in our minds the message
   once the power of God was fully present in the life of man
      and the men who tried could not destroy that power
         goodness and kindness and truth and honor
         are here in the world to stay

men have opposed you with evil and hatred and treachery
   and they are still trying
      they nailed you to a cross and laughed while you died
         but even the power of death yielded to you
            and this was your promise to us
               of the final victory
                  over everything that is wrong with the world

so help us today
   who live in the half-light
      to look forward to the perfect light of your complete victory
      and help us today
         surrounded by those who love the dark
            to let the light of God shine through our lives
            we pray for your sake
                        Amen

FOR CHRIST TO BE INCARNATE IN OUR STRUGGLES

Lord and Master

the power and justice and love of God
   lived on earth when you lived here
      and we crucified you

our minds cannot grasp the mystery of God
   much less can we grasp the mystery of God made man
      walking and talking with his brother man
         sharing our joys and our tears
            knowing our hunger
               our weakness
                  our pain
                     and our fear

forgive us, Lord
   when we try to make our faith a puzzle to be solved
      rather than a life to be lived
         in the light of your glory

thick clouds obscure the light
   clouds of distrust and doubt and fear and prejudice
      habits control our words and our thoughts
         we find it hard to be Christian

you have promised to come to us in the clouds
   come to us today

when we look to you
  we know that the life of faith is possible on earth
  however difficult
    for you have lived here
      despised, rejected, betrayed and crucified
      and triumphant

when we bring you our troubles, we know that you understand
  you have endured sorrow, bless us when we mourn
    you have suffered pain, we offer our pains to you
      you have overcome temptation, help us when we are tempted

you have loved the outsider, the outcast, the person whom respectable
    people despised
  help us to turn to you, not only to meet our own needs
    but for wisdom and strength
      to carry on your ministry of love
        to the unloveable
          we pray in your name

                                        Amen

WHAT CAN I DO BECAUSE I AM SAVED?

eternal Father

you made this world, and all the people in it
   hard as it is for us to understand
     you love the people you have made
      you love the nice, civilized people
        who dress nicely and pay their bills on time
        this we can understand and applaud
        we like to think it includes us

likewise

you love the young people with atrocious manners
   who are experimenting with dope
   and cheapening the mystery of love
   and the way they dress is appalling
     why do you love them?
      simply because you are God

you love the misguided Negro
   who thinks he can build a decent life for his people
   by hatred and violence and destruction
     why?
       you know he's doing everything wrong
        why can't you hate him?
        they way we usually do

you love the Communist
  who is trying to destroy everything we are trying to build
  why?
      he isn't trying to hurry your kingdom along
      he's trying to elbow you out of this world

sharpen our wits a little
  help us to ask the right questions
      why do you love us?
      what can we do because we have begun to respond to your love?

we are like your servant Jonah, who grew jealous and resentful
  when he learned that you loved the people of Nineveh
      help us to do what Jonah did
      he swallowed his pride and told the Ninevites about your love
      he made them listen, and live

give us Jonah's ability
  we're pretty good right now at telling others where they are wrong
      show us how we can help them to be right
      we pray for Christ's sake
                                        Amen

FOR THOSE WHO SUFFER

almighty Father
    you are afflicted in the afflictions of your children
      and are full of compassion
        we pray for your children, our brothers and sisters
        who suffer today

for those who bear the pains of childbirth or sickness

for the aged and the dying

for all who are handicapped in the race of life

for all who suffer injury

for your children who live in darkness

for our brothers who have lost the kindly light of reason

for those who are tormented by nameless fears

for all who long to feel the healing hand of the divine Physician

look on them in mercy
    defend them from danger
      restore to them the joy of your salvation
      in body and in soul
        through Jesus Christ our Lord

                            Amen

THANKS

thank you, Father, for calling us into this world
   at a time like this
     and forgive us, Father
      because we are always
       looking at what's wrong
        instead of looking for what we
         can put right

people in our land, and in every other land
   are threshing about frantically
     because they don't know which way to go
      let alone how to get there

we have caught a glimpse of the eternal light
   help us to walk steadily toward that light
     and perhaps others will learn from us how to walk
      instead of just floundering around

we hold a faith designed to move mountains
   help us to move a few
     indifference, greed, prejudice
      where these things exist in us
       help us to get rid of them
        then we will be able to help others

the world is crying for a savior
   and looking wildly in all the wrong places for salvation

thank you for introducing us to Jesus
   thank you for calling us his hands and his feet
     help us to live our thanks
      instead of just talking about them
       by introducing our neighbors to Jesus
        in whose name we pray

                         Amen

FOR THE COMING WEEK

Savior
we have a whole week stretching ahead of us

help us to try, this week, to be easy to get along with
you know, better than we know ourselves
how grouchy and disagreeable we can be
and you know all the reasons
our aches and pains and disappointments
and the old memories that have left deep scars
the other fellow has troubles too
so help us to try, this week
to be easy to get along with

if we want to bite someone's head off
help us to bite our lips instead

if it is absolutely necessary to say something
the other person will not like
help us to say it so he will know we are trying to help

if we hear something nasty
help us to forget it
or, if we can't, at least not to spread it

help us, when someone asks how we are
to be brief in answering

help us, when we ring someone on the telephone
to remember that we have interrupted
and keep the conversation short

help us, when we want to frown
to remember that a smile is worth more than it costs

help us to pay our bills on time
the other fellow has bills too

help us to be patient, even in a traffic jam
or at least to remember that the horn is designed to prevent accidents
not as a vent for our frustrations

help us to stand up for the right
with courtesy and respect for the person who disagrees
and give us enough sense to know when we are standing for principle
and when we are just being obnoxious

help us, this coming week
to live so that people will know we are friends of yours
we pray in your name

Amen

FOR OUR ENEMIES

you have told us, Father
  to pray for our enemies
    help us to do so
      not just with words
        but with our lives

we know their faults
  we keep talking about them all the time
    we don't ask you to strengthen anyone
      including ourselves
        where he is wrong
          but where there is right
            help it to grow
              even on what we consider hostile soil

where we are right, strengthen us
  where the fault for strife lies in us, correct us
    where we can help those who are wrong to become right
      help us to do our part

help us, each one
  to live at peace with you, with ourselves, and with our neighbors
    help our nation to live at peace with the other nations
      so that we can turn our energy from the tasks of destruction
        to the many crying needs in the world
          we pray in the name of the Prince of peace

                                        Amen

FOR SCHOOLS AND COLLEGES

we pray for a Father's blessing
  on schools and colleges
    on those who teach and those who are preparing there
      you have told us that the truth will make us free
        fill all students and all teachers with a love for truth
        because all truth leads back to you

we pray for those who are leading our country today
  and for those who will be leading our country tomorrow
  asking that they may travel the right direction
    so that our nation may become a land
      whose God is the Lord
        able to help the other nations
          to live together in justice and peace
        we pray in the name of Christ
        the Road and the Truth

                          Amen

FOR TROUBLED PEOPLE

Jesus, friend of troubled people
  we know that you want our friendship
    help us to want yours

we want to keep you boxed up in a quiet hour on Sunday morning
  but you came to be the Lord of life
    the Lord of Tuesday, Wednesday, and Thursday
      the Lord of business, politics, home, school, farm, hospital
        the Lord of our thoughts
          the Lord of our greedy desires
            the Lord of our unruly wills

be our friend on Tuesday and Wednesday and Thursday
  when we are facing tension, anxiety, sorrow, and disappointment
    stand at our side when we are tempted
      you have overcome all the troubles that we know
        we might do better if we faced each trouble with you

you know the rebellion that churns in our hearts
  why must I be honest? no one else is
    why should I be truthful? a little lie won't hurt
      why should I be clean? why can't I do what's natural?
        why should I try to heal the wounds in society? I might get
          my hand bit
            why should I keep my sharp tongue reined in?
              why should I turn the other cheek?
                why? why? why?

you know these questions inside out
you have asked them yourself

you know how dull and unexciting the right can look
you know how, at times, we can fear the right and want to escape it
you know our troubles
you have lived with them

you didn't want to climb the hill to the cross, but you climbed it
and ever since you have been guiding people through life
because you had the courage and faith to do the right
when you wanted to run away

forgive us when we fail to ask any questions about right and wrong
and just plunge ahead, no matter who gets hurt

forgive us when we ask the wrong questions
getting all excited about trifles and calling it Christianity

help us to ask the right questions
help us to find the right answers
and help us to do the right

we pray in your name

Amen

FOR GRACE TO FACE THE FUTURE

father, in your inscrutable wisdom
    you have called us to live in the twentieth century
        when you know well that we want to live in the time of Rutherford
            B. Hayes
            thinking, in our colossal ignorance of history
                that life was easy and simple then
                    and that's what we want, the easy simple life
                    with easy answers to easy questions

since we live in the twentieth century, not the nineteenth
    give us the gumption to admit it
        since the twenty-first century is rushing upon us
        help us to get ready for it

we forget, sometimes, that our fathers looked into a future
    that was filled with uncertainty and fear
        they had to learn how to deal with what was new in their day
        often they made wise decisions
            sometimes they were mistaken
            give us the judgment to decide
                when they were right and when they were wrong

our fathers left us a treasury of experience in business, government, and
    the rest
        we know many tried and true ways of doing things
            that have worked brilliantly in the past
                give us wisdom to recognize what is good in our heritage
                and to treasure it

.

but where the machinery of the past is creaking and groaning
help us to decide if it needs oiling
or if we need new machinery
don't ever let us be in love with the past just because it is past
don't ever let us be in love with what is new just because it is
new

fix our love where it belongs
on the flaming, restless Spirit of Christ
who can never be tied down or embalmed
in any institution or creed or anything else
and yet you have entrusted this Spirit of Christ to us, the church

help us to live in the Spirit of Christ today
confident that he is the Lord of the future
give us wit to keep all that is good from the past
and to discard all that is shoddy
and to build what our children will not need to tear down

Christ is the Carpenter, we are his hands
Father, help us to build
we pray in the name of Jesus Christ, our Lord

Amen

JESUS, WHAT HAVE YOU DONE TO US?

Jesus, what have you done to us?
  we wanted a pet kitten
    and you turned into a tiger
      we liked you the way you were
        why couldn't you leave us alone?

we wanted you to show up when we want you
  to make us feel good
    we wanted a pretty church for weddings and baptisms and funerals
      we wanted the cute Easter bunny hopping around the lawn
      we thought religion is good for the kiddies

now, all of a sudden, you've turned against us
  we wanted peace and you brought us a sword
    things were going along all right
      then you got interested in the poor people
        now they're strutting around like they are going to inherit the
        earth

now, all of a sudden, you tell us to love our enemies
  do you know what will happen if we do?
    they'll nail our hide to the wall
      and what will we do then?
        keep on praying for them?

we liked you when you were a little baby
   gentle, meek, and mild
      cooing in your cradle
         all those nice shepherds and angels
            and we felt just awful about King Herod

look at all we did for you
   we made a national holiday in your honor
   we built big industries around it
      Christmas cards, toy machine-guns for the kiddies
      all those fancy gift-wrapped whiskey bottles

we built pretty churches in your honor
   stained glass, organs, the works
      and when the people moved away from the riff-raff
      the church followed them
         straight out into the suburbs

look at all we've done for you, Jesus
   why can't you leave us alone?
      we've got enough troubles now
         why do you keep poking us in the conscience?
         what do you want, our hearts?

                          Amen

Reprinted through the courtesy of **Presbyterian
Life,** in which this prayer first appeared.

FOR THE CAPTIVES

Lord Jesus
    you came to liberate the captives
        we pray for our brothers and sisters
          who today are in captivity

we remember with pain and sorrow
    our brothers who are prisoners of war
        you have promised to be with them even to the end of the world
        help them to know you are there

we pray likewise for those who have been arrested
    and tried and sentenced for the wrongs they have done
        and now are locked up in jails and penitentiaries

we pray for our brothers in many lands
    who have lost their freedom
        help them to look for help in the right direction
          guard them always against the despair
            that so easily can lead them
              to do all the wrong things

we pray for our brothers who are imprisoned by some vicious habit
  keep us from feeling superior to them
        we are supposed to help, not to harm them further
        usually we don't know what's best to do
          help us to find the right thing
          and help our brothers to be free

we pray for our brothers who are so chained by prejudice
    that they cannot see the truth
        remind us, Lord, that we have a few of our own
        set us all free

we pray for all who are shut in by their physical weakness
   so that they cannot get out and about
      doing the things they would love to be doing
         keep reminding us how much a little note or
            a short visit means to them

we pray for all those who are imprisoned behind their own selfishness
   and don't really care
      about the hopes and needs and fears of others
         most of them are bored stiff with themselves
            and they really don't know how to escape into the human race
               you are the Way and the Truth and the Life
                  show us how we can introduce them to you

Lord, you came here so that we might know the truth
   that will set us free
      help us to know the truth and to live it

we pray in your name

Amen

PRAYERS FOR THE CHURCH

AFTER A PRAYER OF CONFESSION

Father

we have confessed our sins
and you have forgiven our sins
don't let us fall back into the old habits
don't let us hate and despise the people who are wrong
show us how we can love them
and help them to be right

with our sins forgiven
we are off to a new start
help us to go in the right direction
with Jesus Christ
who is the Truth and the Life and the Road

Amen

FOR GRACE TO BE PEACEMAKERS

Savior

help us to be peacemakers
we are so little and the quarreling world is so big
the task is far beyond our strength
but when we stand with you we are with the triumphant majority
keep this faith in our minds when the triumph looks doubtful
your final victory will result from many little victories
help us to win a few of them for you
Lord, make us peacemakers

Amen

Holy Spirit

we know that you will not quench a smoldering flax
  till you bring justice to victory

blow the breath of life on the church
  so that we may no longer smolder but blaze
    and instead of smoke-clouds
      may send out light
        we pray for Christ's sake

Amen

FOR THE NEW YEAR

Almighty God
   our help in ages past
      our hope for years to come
         today, when one year shades into another
            we come with thanks for the good that the year has brought
            and sorrow for the opportunities we have bungled
            and a prayer for strength next year

thank you, Father, for family and friends
   thank you for our work
      thank you for the land we live in, with its tradition of freedom
      and justice
         thank you for our daily bread — why have you given us so much
         and others so little?
         and thank you most of all for yourself
            we don't need to go it alone through the tangle of life

we have not always used your gifts wisely or in the spirit of love
  we have, too often, lived for things and forgotten about people
    we have believed the worst about others, without getting all the facts
      we have spread bad news without checking its accuracy
        we have belittled your children because of their race
          we have failed to express our love
            sometimes we have failed to love
              forgive us, Father

now, with another year rushing upon us
   shine like a pillar of fire in the dark sky
   and show us which way to go
      help us to look to Jesus, every day
      he has called us to follow him
         help us to do it during the year that lies ahead

we pray in the name of Christ our Lord

                                Amen

PALM SUNDAY

Lord Jesus

we remember gladly the timeless story
    how you rode into Jerusalem on a borrowed donkey
    and your friends threw their clothing in the path
    and little children waved palm branches
        it was all very pretty
        and long ago and far away
            forgive us, Lord, for trying to keep it that way

suppose you rode into our city today on a Greyhound bus
    would we be shouting your praise?
      or would we be with the other crowd?
      those who decided to get rid of you

do we really welcome you into our attitudes toward other people?
    or do we prefer to get along without your help?
      how about our attitude toward money?
      it doesn't look much like what you said
      in the Sermon on the Mount

do we put first things first
    the way you taught us?
      do we really seek first the kingdom of God?
      or do we chase after
        security and popularity and pleasure and a lot of other good
          things
          and give our Father what time and energy we have left
          over?

help us to ask the big questions, Lord
    and help us to find the big answers
      by joining with the crowd that surrounded you
      on the first Palm Sunday
        shouting that the answer to life's big questions
        lies in you
          we pray in your name

                                  Amen

GOOD FRIDAY

almighty God
    whose blessed son Jesus endured a shameful cross
      for our salvation

help us to ask
    do I need to be saved?
      saved from what?
      saved to what?

we feel quite comfortable as we look around
    at all the bad people in the world
      criminals, gangsters, racketeers
        political tyrants
          greedy, selfish, cruel people
            those living in flagrant vice

in contrast to them we look quite good
    forgive us, Lord, for being so easily satisfied

when we hold our lives up against the life of Christ
    there is much less room for satisfaction
      we are all mixed up about what is important and what is unim-
        portant
      we are blind to the feelings of others
        we are swift to repeat the nasty rumor
        we are guilty of snobbery and prejudice
        in a thousand subtle forms
          we trust in earth rather than heaven

when we look at ourselves seriously in the light of Christ
    we see that we need far more than a few brave resolutions
    if we are to live we must be born again

we know that Christ offers life
    spiritual life, eternal life
      to everyone who believes in him
        this offer is extended to us
        as well as the down-and-outer

help us never to be satisfied until we are saved indeed
    with the Spirit of Christ filling
      every nook and cranny of our souls
        driving out every habit and attitude that is unworthy of him
        and giving his strength to us
          we pray in his name
                        Amen

EASTER

Eternal Savior

keep the Easter message in our hearts every day
   once, 19 centuries ago, heartless men betrayed you
      they arrested you, tried you, crucified you, and laughed while you
         died
         your friends who wept and your enemies who laughed
            agreed on one thing — you were out of the picture forever
         and that was the day before the Resurrection

keep the Easter message in our hearts every day
   we face the mystery of the Resurrection with humility and awe
   we don't know what happened, much less how it happened
   we cannot explain, but this we know
      men tried to destroy you and they could not
      you lived the first Easter and you live today

keep the Easter message in our hearts every day
   when our hearts are heavy laden because of strife among the nations
   when we are full of uncertainty and fear in all our big cities
      when men of good will disagree violently about the right thing
         to do
      when men of ill will are trying still to destroy you

keep the Easter message in our hearts every day
   we have almost forgotten how to hope
      we are tempted to forget about charity, and to hate those who hate
         us
         our faith gets to be something we apply on Sundays if we feel
         like it

keep the Easter message in our hearts every day
  you are at work in the world
    you want to be the friend of every person here
      sharing our joys and hopes
        guiding, encouraging, restraining, forgiving
          yours is the final victory
            when we are with you, we are part of the victory

keep the Easter message in our minds every day
  while we are at work, while we rest, while we play, while we worship
    whatever we do, help us to remember that you are in the world to
        stay
      whatever we are doing, help us to do it with you
        in your name

                                        Amen

PENTECOST

Spirit of the living Christ
    you are so close that we do not recognize you
      and so we try to make you an unfathomable mystery
        instead of welcoming you as the light and warmth of our lives

you care for each of us as if there were no other person in the world
    yet you care for the whole world as deeply as you care for each of us

since we keep telling ourselves that we cannot find you
    help us to recognize you when you find us
      crash through the brambles and thickets that surround our souls
      clamber over the prejudices and attitudes that bar you
      and find us, here, today

find us through forgiveness
    let us do more than mumble a few words of confession
    give us the experience of coming clean with you
    and finding you ready to cleanse us

find us through conscience
    let our conscience be more than feeling bad when we get caught
    make us sensitive to the right we can do
    and when our desires are wrong, let us know it
    and help us, when our consciences actually work
    to recognize you, God, working in us

find us through guidance
    we think and plan, using the brains you have given us
        we read our Bible and we pray
            opportunities come for us to do the right thing
                when we do it, remind us to give you thanks

long ago you found the church on earth
    our fathers saw tongues of flame and were filled with power
        today the church is rich and well organized
            and we wring our hands because we are so weak
                ignore our constant plea for the easy life
                    and give us strength to do what needs to be done

when we are acting like Christians
    genuinely representing Christ in the community
        teach us to recognize you, the Holy Spirit
            the third Person of the Holy Trinity
                not up in heaven somewhere
                    but in us
                        we pray for Christ's sake

                                            Amen

THANKSGIVING

Father, we give you our bewildered thanks
  why have you given us so much, and others so little?
    why are we privileged to live in a land dedicated to freedom?
    why are we entrusted with so many good things?
    why are we privileged to know Jesus Christ?
    we don't know why, Father
    but we give our thanks

for every deliverance from pain
  for every deliverance from temptation
  for every deliverance from doubt
    for every deliverance from fear
    Father, we give you our thanks

we thank you for the love that brought us into the world
  we thank you for every trace of human love and friendship we have
  known
    we thank you for our opportunities in education and work
    and in our better moments we thank you
    for your guiding hand through the dark valley
    and the eternal light we could see
    only when lesser lights were dimmed

let us never grow smug in our gratitude
  others, as deserving as we are, don't have the blessings we have re-
  ceived
    your gifts aren't rewards for our good behavior
    you have entrusted them to us
    because you are God
    and because we are here to be your servants

thank you for every chance that comes for us to serve you
  sometimes in little ways that nobody notices, except you
    and sometimes in big ways, where we are tempted to bask in the
    spotlight
    whether the opportunity looks big or little to us
    it is our chance to act like Christians
    for which we give our thanks

help us tomorrow to live our gratitude
  as today we pray our gratitude
    in the name of Jesus Christ our Lord

        Amen

ADVENT

thank you, Father
  that into this world
    torn by envy, prejudice, and greed
      the Lord Jesus Christ has come

we are grateful for the memory of his birth
  and all that it has meant to us
    for the laughter of little children
      for the joy that comes from giving rather than getting
        for old friendships renewed and new friendships made

we are grateful for the deeper meaning of Christmas
  that divine strength has entered the world
    to overcome human weakness
      that divine love is the conquering force
        not human hatred
          that through the lowering storm cloud
            the unquenchable light is shining

help us, Father
  bewildered as we are
    to walk by the light that is given to us

Jesus was born in a stable
  help us to care about the lives and hungers and diseases
    of little children everywhere
      Jesus belonged to a despised minority
        help us to care about those who differ from us in any way
          Jesus was a laboring man
            help us to care about the struggles of those who toil
            Jesus came to be Prince of peace
            help us to be peacemakers

the task is so great
  our strength is so small
    yet we rejoice that we can come to you
      in the name and in the strength
        of Jesus Christ our Lord

                        Amen

CHRISTMAS EVE

Light of the world
    whose glory shone on the hills in Palestine
      shine in our hearts tonight
        help us to know the peace that passes understanding
        and help us to bring that peace to others

renew in us the Christmas faith
      renew in us the charity that Christmas is supposed to bring
      so that we will believe in, and hope for, and work for
        brotherhood, righteousness, and mercy

fill our hearts tonight with the Spirit of Christ
    so that no selfishness may dwell in them
    and no folly may blind us to the glory
    of the life you desire for us

visit with Jesus' sympathy
    all who are lonely and afraid at Christmas time
      who look with envy on the happiness of others
        give them the strengthening knowledge
          that Jesus Christ is here, and wants to be their friend

impart the strength of Christ
    to all who battle with temptation

shed through the whole world
    Jesus' spirit of friendliness
      until the ancient hatreds are forgotten
      and the lingering prejudices disappear
        and none of your children must live in want
          because all mankind bows before the Prince of peace

we call our Savior Emmanuel
    and at Christmas we remember that it means
      God with us
        help us to live so that others
          seeing us
            may know you
              we pray in the name of Jesus Christ, our Lord

                    Amen

CHRISTMAS

Christ, whose glory fills the skies
    fill our hearts with your glory

long ago the angels told the shepherds
    that you had come to make a difference in our human lot

today the angels' song is almost drowned out
    by the clack of the typewriter
      and the noise of traffic
        and the radio's blare
          and the distant sound of falling bombs

waken our sleepy hearts
    we have heard the angels' song
      and are supposed to be delivering the message
        that God cares

we are grateful for the eternal miracle of Christmas
    that divine love has entered fully into human life
      forgive us, Lord, if sometimes we think you are far away
        you are always close, you came to us as a baby
          through your life we see the miracle that is possible in every
            life
          your growth shows us how we all ought to grow
           help us to grow that way
             in charity toward our neighbors
             and in love for our Father

we pray your blessing for our neighbors
    to whom Christmas is just a day off
      the ones who never had a chance to know you
        and the ones who had the chance but didn't take it
          where it is our fault that others are hostile and indifferent
          forgive us, Lord Jesus, and put us right
            and help us to work for you instead of against you

help us to express our thanks for the miracle of Christmas
    not just once a year with parties and gifts and excitement
      but every day by quietly living the life
        you came to give to the world
          we pray in your name
                        Amen

ON SATURDAY NIGHT

help us tomorrow, Father
  to worship in spirit and in truth

we pray for a Father's blessing
  on our brothers in faith
    throughout this vast and needy world
      asking that wherever the prayer of faith rises up
        you will be present
          to strengthen and to encourage
            especially do we pray for our brothers
              whose lives are in danger
                because they look to you
                  through Jesus Christ

                                          Amen

PRAYERS FOR ME

blessed Savior
  who endured forty days and forty nights in the wilderness
    and then stood firm against the tempter
      when I am lonely and tempted to give up
        be my Companion

                      *   *   *   *

Father
  my lips say easily that you are almighty
    and my earth-bound heart is reluctant to believe it
      when the strain of life is more than I can bear
        show me the cold tomb from which Christ rose to triumph
        and let me trust

                      *   *   *   *

you have created this immeasurable universe, galaxy upon galaxy
  help me, a speck of dust living on a speck of dust
    to know your love, greater than all that you have made
      great enough to reach even to me
        and help me to respond to your love

PRAYERS FOR ME

you are the answer to every human problem
  help me to solve my biggest problem
    me

* * * *

Lord
  you have blessed me with a magnificent ability to criticize
    help me to use this gift where it counts
      examining myself

* * * *

Christ: Ruler, Teacher, Guide
  forgive my mad passion to hold the steering wheel
    and make me content to accept your direction for my life

* * * *

Lord, you have commanded me to fear not
  help me
    for I find your commandment hard to obey

PRAYERS FOR ME

while I live on earth
   remind me that my eternal citizenship is in heaven
      guard me against being so wrapped up in my daily toil
        that I forget what I am working for

*   *   *   *

when a door of opportunity slams in my face
   teach me to look for the window that you have opened

*   *   *   *

help me to examine
   my family
      my work
        my politics
          my leisure
            my successes
              my failures
                my everything else
                  through the cross

PRAYERS FOR ME

teach me to shut out
   the clamor and tumult of the noisy world
     so that I can hear you calling
      this is the way, walk in it
       then give me the will to walk

         *   *   *   *

you come to me in bread and wine
   gifts of the rich earth
     steel and gasoline come from the earth too
      when I drive my automobile
       ride always at my side
        and make my driving a blessing to others
        and never a tragedy

         *   *   *   *

if I must sweep the sidewalk
   or carry out the trash
   or wash the dishes
     or be patient with a bore
      or anything else I don't want to do
      let me do it to the glory of God

PRAYERS FOR ME

for my sake you climbed a steep hill
  when the uphill climb is beyond my strength
    give me your hand

                    *   *   *   *

you lived on earth with a human body and nervous system
  you know as well as I do the stress and strain of temptation
    I know the tempter well
      help me to know you better

                    *   *   *   *

Christ
  with the law of kindness on your lips
    guard me against unkind words and unkind silences

                    *   *   *   *

Jesus
  you know the sorrows of an outcast
    hated, feared and despised by men
      help the outcasts today to know your love
        and mine

PRAYERS FOR ME

Jesus
    you know the aching pain of hunger
        strengthen your brothers, my brothers, who hunger today
        where there are ways I can help
        show me how

                *   *   *   *

Christ
    infinite in compassion
        when my neighbors offend me, help me to understand
        realizing that probably I offend them too
        help me to amend the offense in myself
        and to forgive the offense in my neighbor

                *   *   *   *

crucified King
    guide your children who bear the heavy responsibility of government
    and help me, one of the citizens
        always to take my share of responsibility
        for justice and peace on earth

                *   *   *   *

eternal God
    your light shines from all eternity
    and supremely from the life of a man
    who lived two thousand years ago

PRAYERS FOR ME

as the mariner plots his course
  by the light of a distant star
    so may I find myself, each day
      by seeing Jesus clearly

*   *   *   *

Lord, you stilled the wind and waves on Galilee
  I wonder, sometimes, why you don't calm the storms today

when the boat threatens to capsize
  I hear your question
    why are you fearful? you of little faith
      that's my trouble, Lord
        strengthen my faith

*   *   *   *

Father
  you made this world
    with its beauty and harmony
      where seedtime and harvest come on schedule
      and each molecule obeys your will
        may my love for your creation
          always lead me back to the Creator
            I pray in the name of your Son
              who taught me to see your hand
                in the lilies of the field
                  and the birds of the air

FOR THOSE I LOVE

God of love
  let me see your image in those I love
    don't let the irritations of daily life hide our love from me
      of them